MAKING
HEALTHY
F O O D
CHOICES

Food for Feeling Healthy

Carol Ballard

Designed by David Poole and Geoff Ward
Illustrations by Geoff Ward
Printed and bound in China by South China
Printing Company

10 09 08 07 06
10 9 8 7 6 5 4 3 2 1

Library of Congress Cataloging-in-Publication Data

Ballard, Carol.
  Food for feeling healthy / Carol Ballard.
    p. cm. -- (Making healthy food
choices)
  Includes bibliographical references and
index.
  ISBN-13: 978-1-4034-8571-7 (hardback)
  ISBN-10: 1-4034-8571-2 (hardback)
  ISBN-13: 978-1-4034-8577-9 (pbk.)
  ISBN-10: 1-4034-8577-1 (pbk.)
  1. Nutrition--Juvenile literature. I. Title. II.
Series.
  RA784.B263 2006
  613.2--dc22
                                    2006003970

Acknowledgments

The publishers would like to thank the
following for permission to reproduce
photographs:
Alamy Images pp. 17 (Jennie Hart), 30
(Vidura Luis Barrios); Anthony Blake Picture
Library pp. 8 (Maximilian Stock Ltd), 39
(Sian Irvine); Corbis pp. 7 (Ed Bock),
9 (Cory Sorensen), 15b (LWA-Stephen
Welstead), 18 (PhotoCuisine), 22 (John
Heseltine), 28 (David Turnley), 33 (RNT
Productions), 36 (Kimberly White), 46;
Getty Images pp. 4 (The Image Bank/
Larry Dale Gordon), 10 (Photodisc), 12
(Stone/ Kevin Summers), 38 (The Image
Bank/ Juan Silva), 47 (Photodisc); Harcourt
Education Ltd pp. 23 (MM Studios),
35 (MM Studios), 41 (MM Studios), 43
(MM Studios), 45 (Tudor Photography),
49 bottom (MM Studios), 49 top (MM
Studios); Photolibrary pp. 11 (Foodpix/
Brian Hagiwara), 13 (GMBH), 15 top
(Foodpix/ Brian Hagiwara), 31 (BSIP); Rex
Features pp. 21 (NXB), 25 (Sipa Press), 32
(ISOPRESS); Science Photo Library pp. 26
(CNRI), 29 (John Daugherty).

Cover image of kiwi fruit reproduced with
permission of Alamy Images (MedioImages
Fresca Collection).

The publishers would like to thank Nicole
Ann Clark RD for her assistance in the
preparation of this book.

CONTENTS

Any words appearing in the text in bold, **like this**,
are explained in the glossary.

WHY DO WE EAT:
What's Your Favorite Food

Sweet and sour, bitter and salty—we all have our favorite foods, as well as those we do not like. However, have you ever stopped to wonder why we eat?

Food is essential for the body. Everyone likes to feel good, and a healthy body certainly helps you to do so. Good **nutrition** is essential for strong bones and muscles, clear skin, healthy hair, and having enough energy to enjoy a wide range of activities. Feeling tired and lacking energy is often a result of poor nutrition. Food plays an important part in helping your body to function properly so that you feel good and look good. Understanding your food will help you to make healthy choices.

▼ Many special occasions, such as birthdays and Thanksgiving, are celebrated with a special meal.

Food and drinks supply the energy our bodies need for activity. They also provide all the **chemical** building blocks our bodies need to grow. These building blocks help to repair our bodies. They replace blood **cells**, skin, hair, and nails and repair damage, such as cuts, bruises, and broken bones. Other chemicals in our food and drinks help us to stay fit and healthy.

FOOD AND SPECIAL OCCASIONS

Food has also become important in other ways. There are often traditional foods to accompany special occasions, such as birthdays and weddings. Religious celebrations and other special events during the year are often accompanied by certain foods—for example, cakes with candles at birthdays, chocolate eggs at Easter, or turkey at Thanksgiving.

Eating food that we like can be a real pleasure, and sometimes we eat when we are not hungry, just to enjoy the taste. Foods, such as ice cream, candies, and chocolate, are often eaten purely for the pleasure they give us.

For a healthy body, you need to make sure you eat the right sorts of food. However, food has also been used in other ways—for example, to try to look good. Here are just a few things people have tried:

- Rubbing avocado onto skin to keep it smooth and soft
- Applying face masks containing oatmeal
- Putting a thin slice of cucumber on each eye to help tired, puffy eyes
- Massaging the body with olive oil
- Placing a warm, used teabag on a pimple
- Rinsing hair in vinegar to make it shine.

Cleopatra, a queen who ruled ancient Egypt, is even supposed to have used milk instead of water in her bath to keep her skin soft! Some of these ideas may have a scientific basis. For example, avocado is rich in vitamin E, which helps to moisturize the skin. Other food-based beauty products may just feel nice without doing any actual good, such as a chocolate bubble bath!

Try an avocado face treatment!

Remove the skin and pit from a ripe avocado. Mash the flesh into a soft pulp. Spread this over your face and leave for fifteen minutes. Rinse twice—first with warm water and then with cold water. Your skin should feel great!

WE CAN'T LIVE ON MILK FOREVER!

The amount and type of food that our bodies need do not stay the same throughout our lives. Changes in our bodies and in our activities mean that our energy needs and some of our food needs are different at different stages in our lives.

BABYHOOD

A newborn baby is fed on milk only. This may be milk from its mother or a specially prepared formula from a bottle. Milk provides everything that a baby needs to grow. In addition a mother's milk provides special chemicals that can help to protect her baby from some illnesses. A baby needs to be fed at regular intervals, often throughout the day and night. After a few months, the baby can be given some soft foods and then eventually progress to eating solid foods.

CHILDHOOD

Many children are very active. Running around, riding bicycles, swimming, and other activities all use a lot of energy, and so children need energy-rich foods. Their foods must also provide all the chemical building blocks needed for growth, since children grow more at this stage in their lives than at any other. Even if children are less active, their foods must still provide all the chemical building blocks needed for growth.

ADOLESCENCE

Many **adolescents** (teenagers) are also very active, either in organized sports or in social activities, such as dancing, so they also have high energy needs. They also often go through "growth spurts," so they still need foods that provide everything needed for healthy growth.

ADULTHOOD

Many adults are just as active as they were in their teens, either from physically demanding jobs or from sports and other activities. They still need plenty of energy-giving foods. Others have less active jobs or get less exercise, and so their energy needs are much lower. Women may need to eat more than usual during pregnancy and breastfeeding.

Although there is no growth during the adult years, bones continue to get stronger until the mid-twenties. Throughout adulthood, it is still important to eat foods that provide the chemical building blocks for maintaining strong bones and muscles and for repairing damage. Eating healthy foods can also help to reduce the risk of problems, such as blocked **arteries**, heart disease, and some forms of cancer.

▲ Our bodies have different food needs at different stages of our lives. Whatever your age, making healthy food choices is important.

OLD AGE

In old age most people are less active than in their younger years, and so their energy needs are reduced. There is no growth, and even replacement and repair slows down, so their overall food needs are also reduced. However, elderly people need to make healthy food choices to stay fit and well for as long as possible.

Calories are a measure of how much energy is in food. The table below shows how our energy needs change during our lives. This is a rough guide. Energy needs will also depend on a person's sex, height, weight, and lifestyle.

Age in years	Average daily number of calories (kcal) needed
2	1,000
5	1,000–1,400
8	1,400–2,000
12	1,600–2,400
15	boys: 2,200–3,000 girls: 1,800–2,400
20	men: 2,600–3,000 women: 2,000–2,400
30–50	men: 2,200–2,800 women: 1,800–2,200
75+	men: 2,200–2,400 women: 1,600–2,000

WHAT IS IN MY FOOD: ?
What Your Food Provides

Different foods and drinks not only look different, smell different, and taste different, but they also provide your body with different things.

The parts of your food that your body can use for energy, maintaining health, or growth and repair are called **nutrients**. There are two groups of nutrients: **macronutrients** and **micronutrients**. Macronutrients provide all our energy as well as most of the substances we need for strong, healthy bodies. They can be split into three groups:

- **Proteins**
- **Carbohydrates**
- **Oils** and **fats**.

However, we do not just need macronutrients to stay healthy. We also need micronutrients. These are just as important, but are needed in much smaller amounts. Micronutrients are:

- **Vitamins**
- **Minerals**.

Some foods contain things that are not nutrients, such as **fiber** and water.

PROTEINS

Proteins are large, complicated substances. They are made up from smaller units called **amino acids**. Your body can break down proteins and then reuse the amino acids, stringing them together in many different ways, like beads on a necklace, to make new proteins. Your body can make some amino acids, but it cannot make them all.

▲ These foods are all good sources of protein.

The amino acids it cannot make are essential for health, so you need to make sure you get 10-35% of your calories from protein.

Every single part of your body needs proteins. Your blood, hair, teeth, muscles, organs, skin, and bones contain protein. Without proteins, your body cannot grow and it cannot repair damage such as cuts or broken bones. It also cannot replace worn-out parts, such as hair and old blood cells, and it cannot stay healthy. Proteins are essential for all-around health.

FOODS RICH IN PROTEINS

Proteins are found in many foods, but some contain more than others. Meat, fish, and eggs are all excellent sources of protein. However, many people are **vegetarian** and do not eat these foods. They can get their protein from other sources, such as **pulses**, which include lentils, garbanzo beans, and other beans. Tofu is also a protein-rich food that vegetarians can enjoy, as are nuts and dairy products, such as cheese and milk.

▶ Protein is an essential part of our diet. It helps to build strong bones and muscles.

Protein supplements

✔ Protein supplements are sometimes taken, usually in liquid form. Some people, such as weightlifters, want to be as strong as possible, so they use protein supplements to help them build up extra muscle.

✔ By choosing the right foods, though, you can make sure that you get plenty of protein for whatever activity you want to do. This is much better for your growing body than using artificial supplements.

✔ Some groups of people should definitely not take protein supplements, since they can harm their bodies. For example, excess protein can cause stress to the kidneys, so protein supplements may be particularly damaging to anyone who has a kidney problem.

CARBOHYDRATES—ENERGY FOR LIVING!

Carbohydrates are good for you because they are important energy providers. There are two main types of carbohydrate: **starches** and sugars. They are found in most foods. However, some carbohydrate-rich foods are healthier choices than others.

STARCHES AND SUGARS

Starches and sugars are related to each other chemically. Sugars are often called simple carbohydrates because they are just small units. When your body digests them, energy is released into your bloodstream very quickly, so you get a rapid response. Starches are often called complex carbohydrates because they are made from hundreds of sugar units joined together into long chains. During **digestion** these chains are broken down into separate sugar units. The amount of time this takes depends on how the chains are joined together. The energy from starches is released more slowly than the energy from sugars. This means that, although the response is slower, the energy lasts longer.

Starches are found in foods made from cereal **grains**. They include bread, pasta, rice, and breakfast cereals. Starches are also found in some root vegetables, such as potatoes.

Whole-grain or white?

✔ Brown rice, whole-wheat pasta, and whole-grain bread and cereals are full of nutrients. They are digested slowly, so you feel full for a long time after eating them.

✔ The factory processes needed to make white rice and white flour (for white pasta and breads) remove many of the nutrients. This means that the foods are not as good for you. They are also digested more quickly, so you soon feel hungry again.

► Starchy foods come from cereal crops, such as wheat (shown here).

▲ Starchy foods like these are good for you and help you to feel full for a long time.

Many foods contain sugars. Some contain a natural sugar. Fruits, for example, contain a natural sugar called fructose, and milk contains a natural sugar called lactose. Other foods may have a sugar called **sucrose** added during their preparation or manufacture. Foods that may contain added sugar include jams, cookies, cakes, and some drinks, as well as many popular snacks such as candy, chocolate, and ice cream.

The healthiest sugar sources are fruits, since they are also rich in vitamins and minerals. Other sugar-rich foods are generally less good for your health because they often contain more sugar than your body needs. They may also contain fewer nutrients.

Glycemic Index

Scientists use a scale called the **Glycemic Index (GI)** to rank foods containing carbohydrates. This gives a measure of how much, and how quickly, sugar is released into the bloodstream after eating a particular food. Foods with a high GI value quickly release a lot of sugar. Foods with a lower GI value release smaller amounts of sugar at a slower rate. Foods with a lower GI value are believed to be healthier than foods with a high GI value. This table compares the GI values of some foods, although everyone responds differently to different foods.

GI value	examples of food
low	apples, grapes, brown rice, whole-grain breads, pasta
medium	bananas, dates, pineapples, raisins, granola bars, pita bread
high	popcorn, jelly, white bread, waffles, white rice, potatoes

▲ Fats themselves are not a problem, but the way that we use them can be. Many people use saturated fats for frying food. Fats soak into the food, and so it is easy to eat a lot more fat than you realize.

FATS—FOODS FOR FUEL!

You have probably heard people say that fats are bad for you, but it is not as simple as that. Your body needs some fats to stay healthy. What it does not need is more fat than it can use!

Fats, like carbohydrates, are excellent energy providers. A gram of fat provides 9 calories (kcal) of energy while 1 gram of carbohydrate provides only 4 calories (kcal).

Fats are also important in other ways. They help your body to absorb some types of vitamins. They play an important role in the production of **hormones**, which are the body's chemical messengers. The **membrane** of every cell in your body contains fats. Fats help your nervous system to work properly and also help maintain your body temperature by acting as insulation. Some of the **fatty acids** from which fats are made are essential for health. Your body cannot make them, so your food must provide them.

WHAT IS THE DIFFERENCE BETWEEN FATS AND OILS?

Fats and oils are made up of very similar basic chemicals. These chemicals are put together to make tiny building blocks called fatty acids. Fatty acids can be linked together in different ways. The different ways they are linked mean that, at normal room temperatures, fats are solids and oils are liquids.

▶ Preparing food using unsaturated fats, such as olive oil, is generally better for your health than using saturated fats.

Types of fat

Fats can be found in all sorts of different foods. There are three main types of fat:

✔ **Unsaturated** fats are found in fish and some plant products. Omega-3 fatty acids are found in oily fish, such as salmon, tuna, and sardines. **Monounsaturated** fats are found in cooking oils, such as nut oils, olive oil, and avocados. Sensible amounts of Omega-3 fatty acids and monounsaturated fats are generally thought to be very good for health. **Polyunsaturated** fats are found in vegetable oils, such as sunflower oil. These are less healthy.

✔ **Saturated** fats are found in animal products, such as meat, lard, butter, cheese, and cream. Eating large amounts of this type of fat can cause diseases, such as heart disease, cancer, and diabetes in some people.

✔ **Trans fats** (sometimes known as hydrogenated fats) are found in some margarines and processed foods. They are made when vegetable oils are specially treated to make them solid at room temperature. Although trans fats extend the shelf life of foods, many experts believe they are unhealthy.

MICRONUTRIENTS

Micronutrients include vitamins and minerals. Vitamins are chemicals that we need in tiny amounts to help our body cells function properly. There are thirteen vitamins known to be important for human health. Each is known by a letter. Some are also known by a chemical name.

vitamin	needed for	may be found in
A	development, healthy eyes/vision, skin, teeth and bones, immunity	eggs, milk, carrots, some leafy green vegetables, yellow and orange fruits
B 1—thiamin	good digestion, normal growth	whole-grains, yeast extract, eggs, meat, fish, nuts, pulses
B 2—riboflavin	healthy eyes, good digestion	milk, whole-grains, eggs, yeast, red meat
C—ascorbic acid	healing of wounds, immune system	citrus fruits, tomatoes, some leafy green vegetables, fruit juice
K	blood clotting	liver, some leafy green vegetables

Minerals are chemicals that are found naturally on Earth. They are absorbed by plant roots into the plant. When we eat the plant, or when we eat animals that have eaten the plant, the minerals enter our bodies. Minerals make up about 4 percent of an average adult's body. Most are in the bones and teeth, but some have functions in other body parts.

mineral	needed for	may be found in
calcium	strong teeth and bones, blood clotting, nervous system	milk, cheese, yogurt, broccoli, fruit juices with added calcium
phosphorus	strong teeth and bones, healthy muscles, nervous system	milk, cheese, meat, fish, nuts
iron	transporting oxygen around the body	red meats, some fish, some leafy green vegetables, whole-grains, eggs, pulses
zinc	immune system	meat, pulses, nuts
potassium	functioning of muscles and nervous system, controlling body fluid levels	fruits and vegetables including some leafy green vegetables, lentils, citrus fruits, bananas

► To be healthy we need the vitamins and minerals found in foods, such as these. Vitamins and minerals are needed by every part of your body. Fruits and vegetables also contain a lot of fiber.

FIBER

Fiber is the part of plants that our bodies do not absorb. However, it plays an important part in keeping the digestive system working smoothly. Without fiber, solid waste (feces) moves so slowly through the large **intestine** that it becomes dry and hard. This makes it difficult to push the feces out of the body when you go to the bathroom. This is **constipation**.

Fiber helps feces retain water, preventing them from becoming hard and dry. This means that you do not become constipated. Fresh fruits and vegetables, brown rice, and whole-meal pasta and bread are all good sources of fiber.

WATER

Water is also important for every part of your body. With too little water, you can become **dehydrated**. This makes your heart beat rapidly and makes you feel light-headed, weak, and thirsty. This can be dangerous. It makes sense to drink plenty of water.

▼ Drinking plenty of water is especially important in hot weather and when you are physically active. It replaces water and salts lost by sweating.

A QUESTION OF BALANCE:
Food Groups are the Answer

Now you know all about the nutrients your body needs. But how can you make sure the foods you eat provide the right amounts of each? Knowing about food groups can help you sort all this out.

Doctors and scientists sort food into large groups that take into account the energy and nutrients each food provides, as well as the good and bad effects each food might have on your body.

From this pyramid, you can also see that the biggest portions of food should be from the grains, vegetables, and fruits food groups. You should eat less from the meat and milk groups and eat even fewer oils and sugars.

▲ MyPyramid was produced by the U.S. Department of Agriculture to help people understand federal government food guidelines.

GRAINS

Eat at least 3 ounces (85 grams) of whole-grain cereals, breads, crackers, rice, or pasta every day.

VEGETABLES

Eat lots of dark-green vegetables such as broccoli, orange vegetables such as carrots, and peas.

FRUITS

Eat a variety of fruits, but go easy on fruit juices containing large amounts of sugar.

OILS

Try to get most of your fat from fish, nuts, and vegetable oils.Try not to eat too much saturated fat and cholesterol.

MILK

Choose low-fat or fat-free whenever possible. If you do not or cannot consume milk, choose dairy-free products, such as soy.

MEAT & BEANS

Choose lean meats and poultry. Remember that nuts and pulses are an alternative source of protein.

GET SORTING!

To get all the nutrients you need, you should try to eat something from each food group every day. So, how does the food from your meals fit into these groups?

	grains and starchy foods	vegetables and fruits	meat, fish, and eggs	dairy	fats, oils, and sweets
Sample menu with each food sorted into the correct group					
first course	bread roll	tomato soup			
main course	potatoes	carrots and peas	chicken		
dessert		berries			chocolate cake
drink				milk	

▼ Ice cream is delicious, but it should be regarded as a treat!

Making sure you eat something from each food group is a good start to making healthy food choices. However, the amount you eat of each food type also matters.

Recommended numbers of servings to eat every day

food group	number of daily servings	examples of servings
fats, oils, and sweets	very little	very little
dairy	2–3 servings	1 cup of milk, or 1 yogurt, or 1 small portion of cheese
meat, fish, and eggs	2–3 servings	1 small piece of fish, such as tuna, salmon or 1 small slice of meat, such as chicken, pork or 1 egg
fruits and vegetables	2–4 servings of fruits 3–5 servings of vegetables	1 piece of fruit, such as apple, banana, orange or 1 tablespoon dried fruit, such as apricots, or a glass of fruit juice 3 tablespoons of vegetables, such as carrots, broccoli
grains and starchy foods	6–11 servings	1 piece of bread or half a cup of rice or pasta or 1 cup of breakfast cereal

Try keeping a food diary for a week. At the end of the week, check whether your food provided the recommended number of servings of each food group. If it did, you have been making healthy food choices. If not, can you think about some changes you could make to improve it?

It makes sense to use these guidelines to organize what you eat every day. Whoever you are, and whatever you are doing, they can help you make healthy food choices.

Pimply skin and smelly breath!

Some foods do more than just provide nutrition. They have effects you would prefer to avoid!

✔ Foods that contain a lot of fat or sugar can cause pimples. Saying no to lots of cakes, candy, cookies, chocolate, and fried foods may help you to maintain clear, blemish-free skin.

✔ Foods that contain too much sugar can cause damage to your teeth. Tooth decay and gum disease can cause bad breath. If you want fresh breath, stay away from too many sweet things!

FIT AND ACTIVE

The amount of food your body needs depends partly on what you do. If you sit around all day, your body will need less food than if you are active. To keep fit and healthy, you need to balance what you eat with what you do.

Whatever you are doing, your body needs a certain basic amount of food just to stay alive. Some processes, such as your heart beating and your lungs breathing, continue all the time, whether you are awake or asleep. These **vital processes** all use up energy.

The amount of energy the vital processes use is affected by things you cannot control, such as:

- Gender: On average, men need more energy than women
- Age: On average, after the age of about twenty, you need slightly less energy each year
- Height: On average, taller people need more energy than shorter people.

Scientists have figured out that, on average, a teenage boy's body uses 1,600 to 3,200 calories (kcal) every 24 hours. A teenage girl's body uses less—about 1,600 to 2,400 calories (kcal) every 24 hours. Therefore, just to stay alive, your food needs to provide these amounts of energy every day. If you are very tall or very short for your age, though, you may need more or less than these amounts. Some medical conditions can also affect the amounts of energy your body needs.

If you simply lay in bed resting all day, your body would need very little energy. The more active you are, the more energy your body uses.

Kilojoules and calories

Scientists usually measure the energy we get from food in units called kilojoules (shortened to kJ). Many other people use a different system of units called calories.

Since one calorie is a tiny amount of energy, people actually calculate in thousands of calories (kilocalories, or kcal). To add to the confusion, they usually call these kilocalories "calories"! Most food labels give both measures of energy, but health books and magazine articles usually stick to calories. We also use calories (kcal) in this book.

▲ Storing a lot of fat is not good for your body. The extra weight in these women's bodies can make just walking along a street very tiring.

WOW!
The risk of heart disease is much greater in people with fat stored around the waist than in people with fat stored around the hips!

Some activities, such as watching television, are gentle and do not use much energy. Other activities, such as cycling and swimming, use up a lot more energy.

An ideal balance would be:
Energy used by vital processes + Energy used for activity = Energy provided by food

STORING FAT

If your food provides more energy than it uses, it stores the extra as fat. This can be useful, because it means that, if you have a day when you use more energy than you eat, your body can get the extra from its fat stores. This is okay now and then, but your body will be healthier if you avoid doing this too often.

FOODS AND ENERGY

Different foods provide different amounts of energy. If you know roughly how much energy you need in a day, you can try to make sure that your food choices provide this.

Making healthy food choices involves balancing the energy your body needs with the energy your food provides. Some foods provide a lot of energy, while others provide less.

Scientists have calculated the energy content of just about every type of food you can think of. By comparing the number of calories in different foods, you can easily see which provide a lot of energy and which do not. The higher the number of calories, the more energy the food provides.

You might be surprised by how different the amounts of energy in different foods can be. Even within a single food group, there are low-, medium-, and high-energy foods. For example, in the dairy products group, there are only 100 calories (kcal) in 3.5 ounces of cottage cheese, but about 350 calories (kcal) in 3.5 ounces of cream cheese. In 3.5 ounces of hard cheese, such as cheddar, there may be more than 450 calories (kcal)!

How you cook your food can also affect how much energy it contains. Adding fat to fry or roast food will greatly increase the amount of energy the food provides. For example, 3.5 ounces of boiled potatoes provide 100 calories (kcal), but 3.5 grams of French fries will provide more than three times this amount.

▼ Grilling, boiling, or steaming are much healthier cooking methods because they do not require any fat to be added to the food that is being cooked. These vegetables have been steamed.

Canned fruit can also be surprising. Syrup is just a sugar solution, so canned fruit in syrup will contain a lot more energy than canned fruit in fruit juice. Canned fruit is good for you, but for healthy food choices, try to avoid those that use syrup.

The amount of energy in a serving of food can depend not only on the food itself, but also on how it has been stored. When food is dried, the water is removed. This means that the nutrients in the food are more concentrated—for the same weight, you get only food and no water. This means that while 3.5 ounces of fresh grapes contain 60 calories (kcal), 3.5 ounces of raisins contain 280 calories (kcal)!

▲ Dried foods, such as these fruits, contain more energy and nutrients than the same weight of fresh fruits.

Making sense of energy

1 kcal (called a calorie) is the amount of energy needed to raise about 2 pints (1 liter) of water by almost 2 °F (1 °C).

1 kcal is the same as 4.186 kJ.

To convert quickly from kcal to kJ, simply multiply by four. To convert quickly from kJ to kcal, divide by four. Your answers will not be exact, but they will be a good approximation.

TOO MUCH OR TOO LITTLE:
The Problem of Extremes

Many doctors are worried by the increase in the number of people who are **obese**. There are numerous reports on television and the radio and in newspapers and magazines about obesity, but do you really know the facts?

"Obesity" is the medical term for having an excessive amount of body fat. People who suffer from obesity are said to be obese. The actual amount of excess body fat that results in a person being classed as obese rather than simply overweight varies depending on age, gender, height, and race. However, a guideline that is sometimes used is that people are obese if they weigh 20 percent or more above their ideal weight.

FINDING YOUR IDEAL WEIGHT

Many doctors use a scale called Body Mass Index (BMI), which compares people's height to their weight. Adults' BMI is calculated by dividing their weight (in pounds) by the square of their height (in inches) and multiplying this by 703.

However, a person's BMI can be misleading because muscle weighs more than fat. This means that people with powerful muscles, such as football players and rowers, may be classed as overweight.

For teenagers, however, age is also an important factor. Teenage bodies are still growing and maturing, so the ideal body weight is not necessarily the same as an adult's. The table below shows suggested healthy BMI ranges from ten to eighteen years of age.

If your BMI is within the healthy range for your age and gender, you should not worry about your weight, even if you think you look too fat or too thin. If your BMI is much higher or much lower than the healthy range for your age and gender, discuss it with an adult you trust, such as a parent, teacher, or doctor.

Healthy BMI ranges

age	boys	girls
10	15–19.8	14–19.9
12	15–21.2	15–21.7
14	16–22.6	16–23.3
16	18–23.9	18–24.4
18	18–24.9	18–24.9

WHY DOES OBESITY MATTER?

Obesity is linked to some serious health problems, such as heart disease, high blood pressure, diabetes, and arthritis.

Several factors may be involved in people becoming obese. Eating too much, eating unhealthy foods, and not getting enough exercise mean that people take in more energy than they use up, and the extra is stored as fat. For some people, **genetic** factors and some illnesses may also play a part.

On average, people are heavier now than in previous generations. Simple things such as using elevators rather than stairs, traveling in cars rather than walking, and grabbing quick snacks and fast food have resulted in increasing obesity problems in many countries.

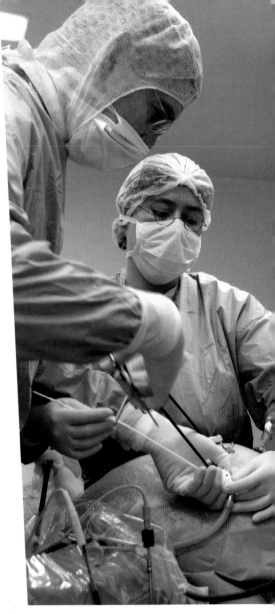

▶ This obese patient is undergoing the drastic step of surgery to staple her stomach. This may reduce the amount of food it can hold and therefore help with weight loss.

OBESITY AND AIRLINES

- It is estimated that passengers' weight gain caused airlines to use 350 million more gallons of fuel in 2000 than in 1990.
- To accommodate the extra weight, airlines are being forced to use plastic knives and forks, to ditch bulky magazines, and to replace the heavy material that makes up seats with more lightweight materials.
- Southwest Airlines charges "customers of size" the price of two seats if they cannot fit into one. This is due to customers complaining about an "uncomfortable" flight when seated next to someone overweight.

In the news

BLACK TEETH AND BLOCKED VESSELS!

For you to stay healthy, your food must supply all the nutrients that your body needs. Did you know that taking in too much of some nutrients can be just as bad as not taking in enough?

A SWEET TOOTH?

People who love sugary foods and drinks often say they have a "sweet tooth"—but it is your teeth that are at risk if you eat too much sugar. Sugar forms part of many snacks, sweets, and drinks. It is in the sorts of things we often enjoy between meals. You usually do not brush your teeth afterward, so tiny amounts of sugar get left around your teeth. **Bacteria** in your mouth feed on these sugars and produce acid. The acid slowly destroys the enamel that makes up the hard outer layer of your teeth. The inner layers of the tooth are exposed and, if nothing is done, the acid destroys these, too. This is called tooth decay, and it can be painful. A dentist can usually fill the hole in the tooth, preventing the decay from getting any worse. If the damage is too bad, though, the tooth may need to be removed.

Fresh fruits and vegetables are healthy food choices for snacks and desserts. The next time you crave a cookie or a chocolate bar, why not try an apple or fresh carrot stick instead?

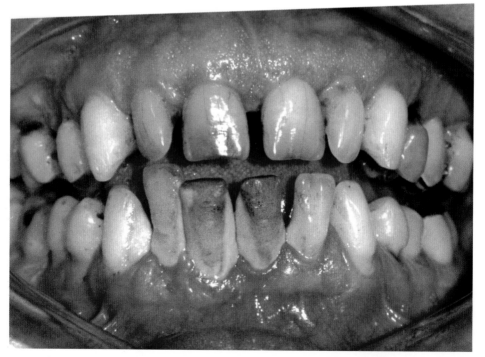

▲ Too much sugar and poor dental hygiene can lead to tooth decay like this!

BLOCKED!

Eating too many of the wrong types of fatty food can be bad for you. The extra fats, along with other bits of debris, can build up on the inside walls of blood vessels. This makes it difficult for the blood to flow through the blood vessels or arteries. A blood clot can build up and block the vessel completely, so that no blood can flow through. Medicines can help to clear the blockages, but sometimes an operation is needed.

Since rice contains much less fat than French fries, it is a healthier food choice. You could eat a crispy fresh salad instead of one with an oily or creamy dressing. Fruit sherbets are low-fat alternatives to ice cream.

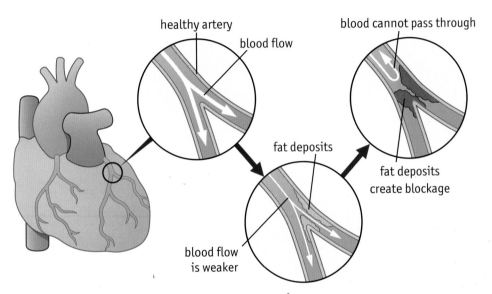

healthy artery

blood flow

blood cannot pass through

fat deposits

fat deposits create blockage

blood flow is weaker

▲ Without treatment, narrowed and blocked blood vessels can cause heart attacks and strokes.

Supplements

✔ Some people like to take vitamin and mineral supplements to make sure they are getting enough of each type. Most of the time, this causes no problems and may be beneficial. However, taking too much of some vitamins and minerals can be harmful. Always check with a registered physician or dietician to see if a vitamin or mineral supplement is needed.

✔ Vitamin D helps to build and maintain strong teeth and bones. However, too much vitamin D can have the opposite effect and actually make bones more fragile.

✔ Iron is needed for transporting oxygen around the body. If you take in a lot more iron than you need, however, it collects in the liver and may damage it and other organs.

▲ These children are suffering from malnutrition. Their bodies do not have the nutrients they need to grow strong and healthy.

MALNUTRITION

Many people in the world do not have enough food to eat. In some countries people do not have enough money to buy food. In others famine may lead to food shortages. Eating too little causes health problems and can eventually lead to starvation and death. Eating too little of a particular nutrient can also lead to specific problems.

"Malnutrition" is the medical name for lack of food. It occurs when a person has had too little protein or energy for a long period of time. A continued lack of protein prevents normal growth and repair processes. Among other effects, it results in a swollen abdomen, tiredness and weakness, and dry skin and hair. These symptoms are seen in many children from famine-stricken areas. Often their only food is cornmeal, which provides carbohydrates, but does not provide enough protein.

A diet that provides too little protein and too little energy will cause health problems. People may become extremely thin and weak, their muscles may waste away, and their skin and hair become dry and dull. These symptoms may be seen in babies whose mothers cannot produce enough milk to feed them and who have no other milk supply. Their food intake is simply not enough for their body's needs. The same symptoms can also be seen in children from areas where there is little clean water and sanitation is poor. The children take in enough food, but chronic **diarrhea** means that it passes through the digestive system so quickly that their bodies cannot absorb the nutrients.

VITAMIN SHORTAGES

In the past, sailors on long-distance voyages spent months at sea without eating fresh fruits and vegetables. Many developed a disease called scurvy. This made their gums bleed and their teeth fall out, and in many cases it was fatal. A doctor found that a daily ration of lime juice could prevent scurvy. It was later found that this worked because lime juice contained vitamin C.

Vitamin D is important for normal bone growth and development. A lack of vitamin D can lead to a condition called rickets. The bones do not harden properly in children with rickets. Leg bones are not strong enough to support the child's weight, so they bend and bow outward.

OUCH!

Sometimes elderly people fall and break a hip. We often think the hip broke in the fall, but in many cases they fell because the hip has given way.

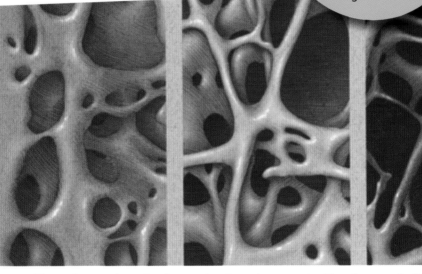

▲ These pictures show the changes in a bone in a person with osteoporosis. On the left is a healthy bone. On the right you can see how the lack of calcium makes the bone increasingly brittle and weak.

Vitamin and mineral deficiency problems

nutrient	some deficiency problems
vitamin A	dry skin, hair, and eyes; poor night vision
vitamin C	scurvy, poor wound healing
vitamin D	rickets
vitamin K	poor blood clotting
iron	anemia
calcium	weak bones, osteoporosis

EATING DISORDERS

An **eating disorder** is a condition in which a person's normal eating pattern is disrupted. Although eating disorders are often thought of as only affecting teenage girls, they can affect men and women of any age. They can cause distress to both sufferers and their families and can have devastating effects on sufferers' health. Most of us skip a meal sometimes or eat too much on a special occasion. This does not mean we have an eating disorder. For some people, though, these patterns become an uncontrollable part of their life.

ANOREXIA NERVOSA

Anorexia is when apparently normal, healthy people begin to deny themselves food. Once this has started, it can be difficult to stop. Sufferers often use subtle strategies to hide the problem from family and friends. These include toying with food rather than eating it, avoiding mealtimes, eating tiny portions, or choosing foods that contain little protein or energy.

Often sufferers believe they look overweight, when in reality their bodies are normal or too thin. They become depressed and withdrawn. As the disorder takes over their lives, their self-image becomes even more distorted, so that they feel a need to become even thinner.

▲ Anorexia can lead to starvation and eventually even death.

"For me anorexia nervosa was an escape route—a way out of the problems I was experiencing. I felt I took up too much space in the world and I needed to slowly and quietly disappear. As I lost weight, I also started to withdraw from the world. My voice became quieter and I never spoke unless I was asked a direct question. I was disappearing into the world of eating disorders, where nothing mattered except food and finding new ways of avoiding meals."

Anna Paterson, www.annapaterson.com

BULIMIA NERVOSA

Another eating disorder is bulimia. Sufferers will often regularly go without food at mealtimes, starving themselves in a similar way to an anorexic. However, they then "binge" in private, in some cases on one particular food, in other cases on any food they can find.

Sufferers regret the binge soon afterward and try to get rid of the excessive food by making themselves throw up, using laxatives, or excessive exercising.

TREATING EATING DISORDERS

Eating disorders are complex conditions caused by the combination of many different factors. Eating disorders are the result of a mixture of psychological

▲ With the right care and support, most people recover from eating disorders with no long-term effects.

causes, such as low self-esteem, lack of self-confidence, anxiety, and stress. Recent research has suggested that there may also be underlying medical conditions.

If family help and support is not enough to guide sufferers back to normal eating habits, therapy in a hospital or special clinic may be necessary. Sufferers may resent this—seeing it more as a punishment than help—but it may be the only way to prevent them from causing themselves permanent harm. There are two main types of treatment:

- Psychological: This helps sufferers understand what they are doing to their bodies and provides ways for them to re-adopt normal eating habits.
- Physical: By ensuring that sufferers take in sufficient food for their body's needs, this can help them to rebuild their body.

In some cases, antidepressants and similar drugs have also been found to help.

FOOD CHOICES:
How Do You Choose What to Eat

Think about the last food that you ate. Do you know why you chose that particular food? Were your friends all eating the same thing? Did somebody else choose it for you? Was it just exactly what you wanted? Was it the only thing in the pantry? Was it the quickest and easiest thing you could find? Once you begin to understand what affects your food choices, you can begin to take more control.

Consider the many different factors that affect our personal food choices.

Peer pressure
This means eating something because people around you—friends or classmates—are also eating it. We often choose the same things as the people we are with. This might be because it is a particularly tasty food, but sometimes it can be because we really want to fit in and be part of the group. If their food choices are not healthy, it is worth making alternative suggestions. For example, if you usually share a bag of chips as you walk home with friends, could you share some grapes or fruits and nuts instead?

Habit
It is easy to get so used to eating a particular food at the same time each day that it becomes a habit. People often eat it without even really thinking about whether or not they really want it. This is normal—for example, many people eat the same thing for breakfast most days of the week. As long as the food is a healthy choice, this does not really matter.

▲ Being inactive and eating lots of snacks, such as chips, dips, and soda are not good for this teenager's health.

▲ These friends are having a great time! However, their popcorn and other snacks are definitely treats to be enjoyed only every now and then.

Comfort eating

Sometimes people eat because they are bored, lonely, or sad. This is called comfort eating. People eat not because they are hungry, but rather just to make themselves feel better. Cookies, chocolate, and chips are common choices, but snacks like these contain a lot of sugar and fat. Healthier choices include fresh fruits, such as apples and kiwis, and dried fruits, such as raisins and apricots.

Circumstances

Most of us will at some time have eaten something we did not really want, just because there was little other choice. Examples might include eating a sandwich with ingredients that are not very healthy, simply because it is the last sandwich in the cafeteria, or skipping a meal completely because you do not have enough money. This does not matter if it only happens now and then, but the healthy choice is to try to make sure it does not happen too often.

Time

If you are rushing to get off to school on time in the morning, you will probably grab the quickest breakfast you can, without thinking about whether it is a healthy choice. In the same way, many people rely on fast food and takeout food, since these take less time than preparing a meal from fresh ingredients. It is better to eat when you are not in a hurry, but sometimes this is unavoidable. It makes sense to try to choose healthy alternatives—for example, a cereal bar and a banana would be a healthier choice for a quick breakfast than a bar of chocolate.

IN THE MEDIA—TRUE OR FALSE?

A lot of information about different foods, drinks, and snacks appears in the media. However, not everything you see, hear, or read is correct. It is important to distinguish information that is accurate from information that is not.

FACT OR OPINION?

When you listen to or read a media report, you need to be able to decide what are facts and what are opinions. Look at these two statements:

A: "Oranges contain a lot of vitamin C."
B: "Oranges taste horrible."

They seem to be saying the opposite. Statement A makes it seem like a good idea to eat oranges, but statement B makes it seem like a bad idea. Which should you believe?

Statement A is a fact. Scientists have measured the nutrients in oranges and proved that oranges do contain a lot of vitamin C. This does not change, and the statement will be true no matter who says it.

Statement B is an opinion. The person who said that probably dislikes oranges. Other people would say that oranges taste delicious. Some media reports are worded so that opinions sound like facts.

BIAS

At a football game, you expect the referee's decisions to be fair to both teams. If the referee constantly gave decisions in one team's favor, it would seem unfair. People would say that the referee was biased.

Media reports can also be biased sometimes. They might only tell you all the good points about something and not tell you any of the bad points. For example, they might tell you how delicious a particular food is and how good it is for your health, but not tell you that it is really expensive.

EXAGGERATION

"I ate so much I was stuffed!" Is this statement really likely to be true? People who say this are trying to stress that they have eaten too much food. They would not really have eaten enough to be stuffed full. Statements like this are called exaggerations—we make something seem much bigger or smaller, or better or worse, than it really is. Media reports can also exaggerate. Headlines are often designed to attract our attention, and one way of doing this is by exaggerating facts.

STATISTICS

Statistics are numbers that are used to back up information, but statistics can be misleading. It is not usually the numbers and calculations themselves that are misleading, though, but rather the way in which they are used. For example, a report might say, "100 percent of people who tasted it loved this dessert." However, unless you know how many people actually tried it, the statistic is meaningless. If only one person had tasted it and liked it, the statistic would still be true, but it gives the impression that the dessert was liked by a lot of people!

▲ Can you distinguish between accurate and inaccurate information in the media?

CLEVER PERSUASION!

Advertisements are all around us—on posters, in neon lights, between television and radio programs, and in magazines. Their aim is to persuade us to buy a particular product, but how do they do it?

▲ Special offers like this can influence our food choices.

The Federal Trade Commission

In the United States, the Federal Trade Commission (FTC) monitors advertising. The FTC says that ads must be truthful and not deceptive, have evidence to support their claims, and not be unfair. The FTC investigates complaints made about false advertising. If you have a complaint about exaggerated claims or something wrong in an ad, you should contact the FTC (www.ftc.gov).

If you wanted to persuade people to buy, for example, a new brand of cookie, you would need to know what kind of people you wanted to sell it to. You could then make your advertisement appeal to those people and try to make sure they would notice it. Using children's television characters, a rock star, or an elderly actor would each make the ad appeal to a different group of people.

The timing and position of ads also matters. You might advertise chocolate in animal shapes during a children's television program, for example. You might put an ad for a healthy yogurt in a lifestyle magazine, while one for baby food might appear in a parenting magazine. Food producers use targeting methods like this to influence our food choices.

ADVERTISING AND STATISTICS

Statistics in advertising can be just as misleading as they can be in media reports. Look at this statement, for example: "9 out of 10 people preferred Brand X." That sounds pretty convincing, doesn't it? However, the advertisement does not tell you what they were given the choice between. If you were asked to choose between fresh bread and a stale, dry crust, you would choose the fresh bread, even if you might actually like another sort of fresh bread more than Brand X.

SELLING STRATEGIES

If you wanted a chocolate bar, how would you decide which one to buy? You could choose your favorite, choose the cheapest, or be persuaded by the color or design of the wrapper. Pricing and packaging can both be used to influence which product you choose.

Free gifts, such as toys inside cereal boxes, can also influence our choices. We can also be influenced by special offers such as "buy one, get one free." An eye-catching entrance display of a product may influence you to buy that instead of another that is in a back corner of the store.

FALSE IMPRESSIONS

Some words or images can be used to create an impression that is not true. For example, showing pictures of cows in meadows or describing food as "farmhouse" is an attempt to give the impression that the food is wholesome and natural. Neither the pictures nor the words really mean anything, but they make us think things that will influence our choice of what we buy.

MAKE THE MOST OF YOUR CHOICE!

You know the types and amounts of food that your body needs to stay fit and healthy, but making the choice to eat those foods is up to you!

When you were a baby or toddler, your parents probably made all your food choices for you. They decided what you should eat, how much, and when. As you grew up, you were probably given more say in what you ate. As you change from a child to a teenager and then to a young adult, your family will expect you to become increasingly independent. This means taking more responsibility for your own life. That includes making your own decisions about what you eat and drink. It is up to you to make healthy choices so that your body can grow and mature properly and stay fit and healthy.

It can be tempting to let friends and classmates influence your decisions, especially if you really like or admire them. However, it is much better to stick to what you know is sensible and good for you. You never know—if your friends see you enjoying a healthy snack, they might decide to do the same! You could also explain why you have made that choice, and why it is healthier than theirs.

▼ The food these girls are eating show some of the healthy choices available in restaurants.

You have already seen how media reports, advertising, and selling strategies are used to persuade you to make particular choices. It is up to you to look at the information and assess what is true and what is false or misleading. Then you can make your choices knowing all the facts.

WHAT WILL I EAT?

You cannot stop to assess information every time your stomach rumbles! Nor can you always stop to think about what your friends are eating or what your family expects you to do. Try to achieve a good nutritional balance

▲ What is in your lunch box? Does it look as healthy and tasty as this one?

over a week as a whole rather than worrying about individual days. To make things easier, you can set out some food guidelines for yourself. Try to make them easy to remember and easy to stick to—otherwise, you will soon give up. What do you really enjoy? Can you combine these foods to give you a healthy, balanced diet? Try to make your guidelines positive. Say, "I will…" instead of "I won't…"

Your guidelines might be something like this.

On schooldays I will try to eat:
- Cereal for breakfast
- Fruit during a morning break
- Chips or chocolate for lunch only on sports practice days
- Whatever the family has for dinner.

This would be quite easy to follow, and it allows you some treats.

Alcohol

Many adults enjoy drinking alcohol. As you grow up, you will need to make your own decisions about it. There are guidelines about sensible drinking levels, and you should try not to exceed them. Too much alcohol can cause serious, often long-term harm to your body. There are plenty of delicious non-alcoholic alternatives, such as smoothies, shakes, and fruit juice cocktails.

FOOD LABELS:
Making Sense of Packaging

Much of our food today is sold in packages, cans, jars, bottles, tubs, and other containers. It is easy to ignore the packaging and just put it in the garbage or recycling can, but if you look carefully you will find that it gives you a lot of information that will help you make healthy food choices.

Most countries have laws that control what food manufacturers put on their food packaging. There are regulations about what they must include as well as what they must not include. The regulations cover pictures, names, information about what the food contains, and instructions for storing the food. In the United States most regulations are controlled by the Food and Drug Administration (FDA).

GOOD LABELING

What appears on food packaging might not seem important to you, but to the FDA it certainly is. The FDA wants to make sure that the information on the packaging does not mislead you about what is inside. All food packaging must contain labels that list the nutritional value of the food. Since 2003 labels must also list any trans fats. To avoid false claims, any health claims made on packaging labels must be consistent with the standards of the U.S. Department of Health and Human Services.

Food packaging must clearly show how much food it contains. For solids this is usually shown as the weight of the solid in ounces, cups, or grams. For some items, such as cookies, the number of items may be shown. For liquids the volume is usually shown in gallons, liters, quarts, or fluid ounces. This information helps you compare different products, especially when you want to know which is the best value.

Storage conditions and defrosting and cooking times are often also included. It makes sense to follow instructions like these. They are there to ensure your food is fresh and safe to eat.

INGREDIENTS LABEL

Ingredients are listed in order of weight, according to the amounts that were used to make the food, starting with the largest ingredient and ending with the smallest. Some ingredients are given as a percentage of the whole.

The **allergy** advice part of the label is the most important for people who suffer from allergies. In granola, for example, a person with allergies might need to watch out for wheat, oats, barley, sesame seeds, or nuts.

In 2004 the U.S. Congress passed legislation that requires all companies to create labels for foods that contain any of the eight most common food allergens (substances that produce an allergic response): wheat, soy, milk, fish, shellfish, eggs, peanuts, and tree nuts.

USE BY:
SEPT 30 06

▲ Food packaging contains instructions about how long food may be stored. This is usually shown as a "best before" date or a "use by" date. Freshly squeezed orange juice will not last as long as juice that has many preservatives added to it.

What are food additives?

✔ **Food additives** are chemicals that are added to our foods. Chemicals must be proven safe to eat before the FDA will allow them to be used as food additives.

✔ Flavorings give food extra flavor and colorings are used to make food look more attractive. Preservatives increase the length of time a food may be stored.

✔ Sweeteners are used instead of sugar to add sweetness without calories.

WHAT DOES A NUTRITION INFORMATION LABEL SHOW?

In addition to the general information on food packaging, details about the nutrients the food contains are often shown. These details are shown on a label called a Nutrition Facts label. Different countries have different regulations about what these labels should show.

Nutrition Facts labels show the amounts of energy and nutrients the food contains. The example below is taken from a package of granola. The information is based on the amount of energy and nutrients that a typical serving would provide. The label also shows the percentage of the Daily Value for each nutrient that a serving of food provides.

Nutrition Facts:

Serving size ½ cup (48g)
Servings per container: about 17

Amount Per Serving:

Calories 195

Calories from Fat 45

	% Daily Value*
Total Fat 5g	**8%**
Saturated Fat 3g	**15%**
Trans Fat 0g	
Polyunsaturated Fat 1g	
Monounsaturated Fat 1g	
Cholesterol 0mg	**0%**
Sodium 25mg	**1%**
Potassium 200mg	**6%**
Total Carbohydrate 32g	**11%**
Dietary Fiber 3g	**13%**
Sugars 12g	
Protein 5g	
Vitamin A	0%
Vitamin C	0%
Calcium	5%
Iron	7%
Thiamin	11%
Phophorus	14%
Magnesium	9%

This row shows how much energy the food contains. Figures are given in calories (kcal). You can use this as a guide to figure out how much energy a meal will give you.

The next section shows the amounts of individual nutrients, in grams.

This row shows how much fat the food contains. The amount of individual fats is shown separately.

This row shows how much sodium and salt the food contains. Sodium may come from added salt or it may be naturally present. Sodium is more concentrated than salt.

On this label, the amounts of sugar and dietary fiber are shown as well as the total carbohydrates. However, on other labels it is not always clear how much sugar is naturally in the food and how much has been added during the production process. The rest of the carbohydrates will be starch.

This section shows the amounts of vitamins and minerals as a percentage of the recommended daily amount for each.

▲ A serving of granola can provide plenty of the nutrients your body needs.

DAILY VALUES

By law foods in the United States must provide information about Daily Values (DVs). Rather than recommended daily intakes, DVs are reference points to help people understand their approximate dietary needs. DVs are given based on the estimated average nutrition needs for people of normal weight and fitness on a 2,000-calorie (kcal) diet. Larger food packages, such as this granola package, also include DVs for a 2,500-calorie (kcal) diet. DVs can help people understand how much of the energy (calories), fat, and salt that they should have in a day are in a portion of food.

* Percent Daily Values are based on a 2,000 calorie diet. Your daily values may be higher or lower depending on your calorie needs:

	Calories:	2,000	2,500
Total Fat	Less than	65g	80g
Sat. Fat	Less than	20g	25g
Cholesterol	Less than	300mg	300mg
Sodium	Less than	2,400mg	2,400mg
Potassium		3,500mg	3,500mg
Total Carb		300g	375g
Dietary Fiber		25g	30g

Ingredients: Whole grain rolled oats, whole grain rolled wheat, brown sugar, coconut oil, nonfat dry milk, almonds, whey, whey protein concentrate, honey, natural flavors, sunflower oil. (676-47)

CONTAINS WHEAT, MILK AND TREE NUT INGREDIENTS

These are the Daily Values of nutrients needed per day based on a 2,000-calorie diet. For example, a person on such a diet needs 300 grams of carbohydrates per day. A portion of this granola will provide 32 grams of carbohydrates. That is around 11 percent of the person's daily need for carbohydrates.

Ingredients are listed in descending order of weight (from most to least).

COMPARING FOODS

When you are standing in a store looking at two tubs of yogurt, how do you decide which is the most healthy? Comparing the information on the packaging will help.

If a food is sold as "low fat," it must contain less fat than a normal food of the same type. For example, a low-fat cookie must contain less fat than an ordinary cookie. It does not give you any idea of the exact amount of fat the cookie contains, though. It could still contain a lot more fat than other types of cookie.

The same is true of foods with labels such as "low sugar" or "reduced sugar." Similarly, foods labeled "high fiber" might not contain a lot of fiber. They just have to contain more than a normal food of the same type.

COMPARING NUTRITION LABELS

The labels below are from two different strawberry yogurts. We have kept only the values for 3.5 ounces (100 grams) of the yogurts. You can compare them line by line to find the differences.

The first carton of yogurt contains more than three times as much energy and more than twice as many carbohydrates as the second. The first carton contains slightly less protein than the second and only half as much fiber. The biggest difference, however, is in the fat content: the first contains 6.9 grams of fat, while the second contains only 0.1 grams.

STRAWBERRIES AND CREAM YOGURT NUTRITION INFORMATION	
Typical composition	**100 g provides**
Energy	575 kJ/137 kcal
Protein	3.4 g
Carbohydrates (of which sugars)	15.4 g 14.8 g
Fat of which saturates monounsaturates polyunsaturates	6.9 g 4.4 g 2.0 g 0.2 g
Fiber	0.5 g
Sodium	0.1 g

▲ Is the yogurt in any two tubs the same? Compare the labels below to find the difference.

Which should you choose? That depends on a whole lot of things, such as your age, how active you are, if you are overweight or underweight, and the other food choices you are going to make for that day. The taste of the yogurt would also affect your decision. Generally, though, a lower-fat, higher-fiber option is considered to be healthier, which would make the light yogurt the healthier choice.

LIGHT STRAWBERRY YOGURT NUTRITION INFORMATION	
Typical composition	**100 g provides**
Energy	175 kJ/41 kcal
Protein	3.9 g
Carbohydrates (of which sugars)	6.2 g 4.3 g
Fat of which saturates	0.1 g 0.1 g
Fiber	1.0 g
Sodium	1.0 g

▲ Compare the nutritional values of a light strawberry yogurt with a strawberries and cream yogurt.

FOOD JARGON—WHAT DOES IT ALL MEAN?

Words like "junk," "fast," "GM," and "**organic**" are used to describe the food available to us. You are in a better position to make healthy food choices if you understand what they are telling you.

WHAT IS "JUNK FOOD"?

"Junk food" is applied to a wide range of foods, and it probably means different things to different people. It is usually understood to mean food that has little or no nutritional value, may contain a lot of fat or sugar, and may also contain many food additives. Foods that are classed as junk foods tend to be snacks and pre-prepared. This does not mean that every snack and pre-prepared meal is junk food. There are a lot of very healthy ones available, but some are definitely better for you than others.

WHAT IS MEANT BY "FAST FOOD"?

"Fast food" is used to describe any prepared food that is ready to eat quickly. This may mean pre-prepared meals that just need to be reheated. It can also mean food that you buy from places, such as burger joints, hot dog stands, and fast-food chains. Fast food often has a high fat content and so is regarded by many people as unhealthy. Some fast-food chains have tried to change this idea by offering a range of salads and other alternatives. However, salads with rich dressing or extras, such as croutons, may still contain the same amounts of fat and salt as other items on the menu.

◀ Meals like this often contain a lot more fat, salt, and additives than are good for your health.

▲ Organic vegetables, like these carrots, can be found in most supermarkets.

WHAT ARE "ORGANIC" FOODS?

To increase the amount of food that can be grown on a piece of land, farmers use chemicals such as weedkillers, pesticides, and some fertilizers. The amounts and types of chemical that can be used on food crops are controlled by strict regulations. The chemicals may do the job very well. However, some people are concerned about the effects these chemicals may have on people who eat the foods, and on the environment.

Natural, chemical-free farming methods are described as organic. Foods produced on organic farms are called organic foods. Scientists and doctors cannot prove that organic foods are better for you than non-organic foods. Many people, however, believe that organic foods are tastier than other foods and also better for your health.

WHAT DOES "GM" STAND FOR?

"GM" stands for "genetically modified." This means that scientists have altered the genetic material of one of the ingredients. For example, the genetic material of some crop plants has been changed to make them resistant to infections and pests, thus reducing the need for chemicals. These GM plants produce a higher yield, and so the crop is cheaper.

Selecting different crops for different properties is part of farming. GM crops are different in that the selection has been done artificially. This may sound like a good idea, but farmers have not been growing GM crops for very long. Therefore, nobody is exactly sure what the long-term effects might be, either on people or the environment.

Some foods are labeled "GM free." This means that none of the ingredients used to make the food have been genetically modified.

RECIPES

These recipes make enough for a main meal for two people. For one person, use half of each quantity. For four people, double each quantity.

Remember these basic food hygiene and safety rules whenever you prepare food:

- Always wash your hands before you begin
- Make sure work surfaces and utensils are clean
- Be careful when using knives and other sharp utensils
- Check with an adult before using the stove
- Avoid leaving **perishable** foods at room temperature. Most are best stored in a cold place.
- Keep raw and cooked meats separate.

Be helpful: leave the kitchen clean and neat when you finish!

PASTA WITH FRESH TOMATO SAUCE

Ingredients:

2 cups whole-wheat pasta

5 ripe tomatoes (finely chopped)

1 teaspoon dried mixed herbs

2 tablespoons grated cheddar cheese (you could use low- or half-fat cheese)

Method:

1. Boil water in a large pan.
2. Add pasta.
3. Cook until tender (usually 12–15 minutes—look at the package for the exact cooking time).
4. While the pasta is cooking, put the tomatoes and herbs into a small pan.
5. Heat gently, stirring occasionally, until boiling.
6. Turn the heat down and simmer gently until the pasta is ready to serve.
7. Drain the pasta and serve into two bowls or plates.
8. Spoon the sauce over the pasta.
9. Sprinkle the cheese on top of the sauce.
10. For a really special look, top with a sprig of parsley or a few fresh basil leaves.

Cooking tip:

Adding a few drops of olive oil to the water before you add the pasta will help prevent the pasta from sticking together.

▲ Pasta with fresh tomato sauce is fast and easy to make.

NUTTY SALAD

Ingredients:
lettuce or other salad leaves
$1/2$ green pepper
1 small carrot, peeled
4 small mushrooms
$1/2$ celery stalk
cucumber
2 tablespoons raisins
2 tablespoons pine nuts

Method:
1. Wash the salad and celery thoroughly.
2. Chop all the ingredients (apart from the pine nuts and raisins) into small, bite-sized chunks.
3. Put the salad into a large bowl and add the pine nuts and raisins.
4. Mix together well.
5. Serve in two bowls or plates.

▲ You can vary the salad ingredients in nutty salad to make a selection you really like.

MENU FOR ONE WEEK

This menu gives some suggestions for healthy breakfasts, lunches, and evening meals each day for a week. You may not want a different breakfast every day or a dessert every day. Canned or frozen fruits and vegetables are healthy alternatives to fresh fruit. If you want a snack between meals, raw vegetable sticks, fresh fruit, dried fruit, and some cereal bars are healthy and delicious.

	Monday	Tuesday	Wednesday
Breakfast	pineapple juice, granola, milk	fresh grapefruit, whole-grain toast, honey	oatmeal, orange juice, banana
Lunch	pasta with tomato and cheese, salad, banana	chicken and lettuce sandwich on whole-grain bread, kiwi fruit	pita bread with lamb and roasted peppers, fruit yogurt
Dinner	baked chicken breast, spinach, ice cream	beef lasagna, salad, baked apple and ice cream	veggie burgers, broccoli, baked potato, fruit smoothie

Good menu planning is based on balancing the foods you eat. Choose the amounts of each type of food using the guide on pages 16–17. When choosing foods, consider the nutrition and calories in each serving. You should also learn about the amount of fat and salt or sodium these foods may add to your daily menu. Read labels and ingredient lists to find out what a product contains.

Try to "budget" the amount of saturated fat you should have. For example, if you eat foods high in salt or saturated fat in one meal, balance them with foods lower in salt and fat for your other meals that day.

Thursday	**Friday**	**Saturday**	**Sunday**
fruit yogurt, bagel, honey	orange juice, granola, milk	orange juice, boiled egg, whole-grain bread	grapefruit juice, blueberry fruit salad, whole-grain toast
baked potato with cottage cheese, salad, grapes	cheese and lettuce on a whole-grain bread roll, grapes	vegetable stir-fry with shrimp, cereal bar	tomato soup, vegetable salad, melon slice
cheese and tomato quiche, salad, baked potato, blueberry tart	grilled tuna, salad, lemon sherbet	chicken and vegetable curry, brown rice, cheese plate	roast chicken, carrots, spinach, potatoes, chocolate cake

GLOSSARY

adolescent person in the years between childhood and adulthood

allergy when the body is sensitive to a particular substance

amino acid chemical substance that occurs naturally in the body and forms proteins

arteries major blood vessels that carry blood from the heart to the rest of the body

bacteria (plural of bacterium) single-celled organisms, so small they can only be seen under a microscope, that can cause illness and disease

carbohydrate nutrient, such as sugar or starch, made from sugar units

cell one of the tiny units from which all living things are made

chemical substance formed by chemistry

constipation condition in which feces are dry and hard and it is difficult to go to the bathroom

dehydrated having too little water

diarrhea condition in which feces are semi-liquid and you need to go to the bathroom a lot

digestion process of breaking food into separate chemicals in your body

eating disorder condition in which normal eating patterns are disrupted. A person may eat too much or too little.

fat nutrient, such as butter or olive oil, made from fatty acids

fatty acid chemical unit from which fats are made

fiber mainly made up of the parts of plants that your body cannot digest

food additive anything added to foods

genetic to do with information being passed from generation to generation via genes, the chemical codes that say what a living thing is and what it looks like

Glycemic Index (GI) measure of how quickly energy is released from a carbohydrate

grain cereal, such as rice, wheat, corn, oats, and barley

hormone chemical released in the body that affects other parts of the body

intestine part of the digestive system that links the stomach to the anus

macronutrients nutrients that the body needs in large amounts

malnutrition poor nourishment resulting from lack of food

membrane (of the cell) outer boundary of the cell that controls what goes in and out of the cell

micronutrients nutrients that the body only needs in small amounts

mineral chemical that is found naturally on Earth

monounsaturated fat with one unsaturated fatty acid

nutrient part of a food that the body can use

nutrition science that deals with the body taking in and using nutrients from food to keep healthy

obese being so overweight that a person's health is at risk

oil fat that is liquid at room temperature

organic food not treated with any chemicals

perishable food that will rot quickly if it is not kept in the refrigerator

polyunsaturated fat with more than one unsaturated fatty acid

protein chemical made from small units called amino acids

pulse food from the legume family, such as peas and beans

saturated fats found in animal foods

starch nutrient made up from tens or hundreds of sugar units

sucrose chemical we usually call sugar

trans fats when liquid vegetable oils are treated so that they become solid at room temperature. They usually melt at body temperature.

unsaturated fats found in fish and some plant products

vegetarian person who does not eat meat

vital process process that is essential for life—for example, the heart beating

vitamin substance needed in small amounts for normal growth and development

FINDING OUT MORE

You can find out a lot more about healthy food choices from books, encyclopedias, and lots of different websites. Some starting points are listed below.

LOOK CLOSELY AT LABELS

The next time you are in a supermarket, check out some of the labels and compare different brands for ingredients and nutritional value. Which are the best value and which are the most healthy?

BOOKS

Body Needs series: Titles include *Carbohydrates for a Healthy Body, Fats for a Healthy Body, Proteins for a Healthy Body, Vitamins and Minerals for a Healthy Body,* and *Water and Fiber for a Healthy Body.* Chicago: Heinemann Library, 2003. This series looks at what the human body needs to function healthily.

Buller, Laura. *Food.* New York: Dorling Kindersley, 2005.

Davidson, Alan. *Penguin Companion to Food.* New York: Penguin, 2002.

Kedge, Joanna, and Joanna Watson. *Teen Issues: Diet.* Chicago: Raintree, 2005.

Morgan, Sally. *Science at the Edge: Genetic Modification of Foods.* Chicago: Heinemann Library, 2002. Learn more about genetically modified foods.

Townsend, Sue, and Caroline Young. *A World of Recipes: Vegetarian Recipes from Around the World.* Chicago: Heinemann Library, 2003.

Warbrick, Caroline. *Just the Facts: Eating Disorders.* Chicago: Heinemann Library, 2003.

WEBSITES

www.usda.gov

This is the site of the U.S. Department of Agriculture (USDA), which is responsible for food and nutrition in the United States.

www.fda.gov

This is the site of the U.S. Food and Drug Administration, an agency of the U.S. Department of Health and Human Services.

www.mypyramid.gov

This USDA site offers information on the food guide pyramid, MyPyramid.

www.nationaleatingdisorders.org

This is the website of the National Eating Disorders Association. This site lists different programs, books, and phone numbers you can look into to get advice or help.

www.foodallergy.org

This website provides education, advocacy, research, and awareness about food allergies.

www.ams.usda.gov/nop

This section of the USDA website, part of the National Organic Program, offers information on organic food and farming.

FURTHER RESEARCH

If you are interested in finding out more, you can research the following topics:

- How the digestive system works
- How foods, such as bread and pasta, are made
- Using foods as beauty treatments
- Where different foods come from.

INDEX